The Teaching of Shorthand

You are holding a reproduction of an original work that is in the public domain in the United States of America, and possibly other countries. You may freely copy and distribute this work as no entity (individual or corporate) has a copyright on the body of the work. This book may contain prior copyright references, and library stamps (as most of these works were scanned from library copies). These have been scanned and retained as part of the historical artifact.

This book may have occasional imperfections such as missing or blurred pages, poor pictures, errant marks, etc. that were either part of the original artifact, or were introduced by the scanning process. We believe this work is culturally important, and despite the imperfections, have elected to bring it back into print as part of our continuing commitment to the preservation of printed works worldwide. We appreciate your understanding of the imperfections in the preservation process, and hope you enjoy this valuable book.

The
Teaching of Shorthand

SOME SUGGESTIONS TO YOUNG
TEACHERS AND OTHER
ADDRESSES

BY
JOHN ROBERT GREGG

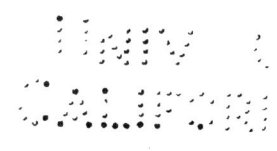

THE GREGG PUBLISHING COMPANY
NEW YORK   CHICAGO   SAN FRANCISCO

COPYRIGHT, 1916, BY
THE GREGG PUBLISHING COMPANY

G89

CONTENTS

	PAGE
THE TEACHING OF SHORTHAND: Some Suggestions to Young Teachers	1
THE ART OF TEACHING SHORTHAND	31
"TRICKS OF THE TRADE" IN TEACHING SHORTHAND	57
EFFICIENT STENOGRAPHERS: What Should Their Attainments and Qualifications Be when They Graduate from the School	83
THE APPLICATION OF MODERN EFFICIENCY PRINCIPLES TO THE TEACHING OF SHORTHAND	101

460978

THE TEACHING OF SHORTHAND

SOME SUGGESTIONS TO YOUNG TEACHERS

An Address to the Students in the Summer Normal School for Shorthand Teachers Gregg School, Chicago

THE TEACHING OF SHORTHAND

IN teaching the theory of shorthand, as in teaching all other subjects, there are three main divisions:

1. THE PRESENTATION, or explanation of the lesson.

2. THE APPLICATION, or practice of the examples for the purpose of deepening the impression and developing skill.

3. THE EXAMINATION, or test for the purpose of ascertaining the results of the instruction and practice, and for the guidance of the teacher in assigning work.

These three processes are closely connected, and when properly applied they result in knowledge, power and skill. In each of these divisions you can apply an infinite variety of methods.

The Teaching of Shorthand

Let us consider these processes in the order I have given them.

THE PRESENTATION

A wide difference of views and methods exists in regard to presentation. Some teachers hold that the entire lesson should be explained in detail before the student is allowed to proceed with the study or practice of it; others maintain that no explanation should be given, as the student will have the principles more thoroughly impressed on his mind by working them out for himself, and, in addition, will acquired self-reliance by so doing.

The great Pestalozzi says, "Never tell a child what he can find out for himself," and Herbert Spencer expresses the same thought, but not so sweepingly, when he says, "Students should be taught as little as possible and induced to discover as much as possible."

When Philip of Macedon presented his son, who afterwards became Alexander the Great, to Aristotle as a pupil, he said, "See that you make yourself useless to my son." A great teacher, using this expression as a text, has said: "Teach your pupils to think, show them the sources of information and teach them how to use those things with which they will have to do, and you have done more for them than you could possibly have done by cramming their minds with a thousand facts, useful though they may be."

But in connection with these wise maxims it should be borne in mind that the acquirement of shorthand involves not merely an intellectual understanding of rules and principles, but actual *manual skill* in execution, therefore this theory of education should not be given too literal an application to shorthand instruction. Shorthand is *largely manual*, and the technique of execution can be most quickly secured by the imitation or practice of correctly written forms placed before the student as illustrations. For instance, when you place a shorthand form on the board, your students instinctively imitate your manner of writing and the actual form of the word or phrase.

Therefore between these extremes, of an exhaustive explanation of the lesson and no explanation whatever, I take the middle ground.

I believe that the teacher can best secure the attention and gain the confidence of the student by a brief but interesting and helpful explanation of the most important features of each lesson. I believe thoroughly in laying great emphasis on making the lessons *interesting*. Where you secure interest you are bound to secure deep impression. Without the cheerful, magnetic influence of the teacher, there is always an atmosphere of discouragement in the shorthand classroom. A well-known teacher in discussing this subject said: "Some teachers make the mistake of requiring the student to dig his own way through the theory. Much valuable time is thus lost, and not a thing is gained. Interpret the author's text for the pupil, and get him to the main business of his course, *writing*, without a moment's delay."

In giving such an explanation there is no more helpful adjunct than a good blackboard. It is a pity that the value of blackboard work in teaching shorthand is not more fully realized. By the skillful use of the blackboard at all stages of shorthand study an energetic, resourceful teacher can most effectively arouse the interest and enthusiasm of the students, and secure satisfactory results. I most earnestly urge that you see to it that you have a good blackboard and the best chalk obtainable, and further that you practice assiduously to acquire a style of writing that will be an inspiration to your students.

Get close to the students. If the blackboard is a wall fixture around the room — intended more for decorative purposes or the display of fancy penmanship than for actual service — and is at some distance from the first row of students, then by all means make other provision. Get a board on a stand if necessary, but get a board that you can use at all times *close to the students*, so that they can clearly see the shorthand forms, and where they are distinctly within the range of your influence.

Having assembled your class in seats in front of the blackboard, the first thing is to secure *undivided attention*. To do this without apparent effort, is an art in itself — an art that is worth all the attention you can give it. Without close attention, you cannot hope for satisfactory results. There are many ways of securing attention, but I believe in the *quiet* method. If the teacher will merely stand before the class for a minute or two looking at the students quietly and steadily, without uttering a word or manifesting impatience or nervous hurry, absolute silence and attention will be secured — provided the teacher has the respect and confidence of the students.

Begin quietly by asking them to open their books at page so-and-so, if they have not already acquired that habit. Say, "If you will give me your attention for a few minutes, I will explain the first principles of the lesson you are about to study" — or something of that kind.

Having explained the first rule or principle, place the illustrations on the board. As far as possible make use of illustrations *not given in the book* (your students will learn what is in the book by personal study) as this will give additional interest to your remarks, and secure for them more attention, because new words under a principle have a power of stimulating interest that leads to deep and lasting impression. The words thus selected, too, should be *common* words so that the student will be continually adding to his stock of useful shorthand forms. The application of the principles to new words will also show reserve power and knowledge outside of the text-book, which will inspire respect and confidence.

It may be asked, "What purpose is served by giving explanations and illustrations of rules so fully explained and illustrated in the text-book?" The chief purpose is to make a *vivid* impression on the memory of the student, who will remember the teacher's oral explanation and the blackboard illustrations long after the text-book rules and illustrations have faded from his memory.

To quote from an address I made to teachers some years ago:

"I believe the teacher should be superior to the text-book, just as the finished actor rises above the written play. We read a play, and find it dull and lifeless; but when we see it interpreted by a great actor like Mansfield it makes a vivid impression on our minds. So it is in teaching shorthand. Our pupils, being young, do not realize the necessity for careful preparation, and are likely to slight the lesson unless the teacher, by his personal force and the use of the blackboard, interests them in it.

"I think, then, there should be some presentation of the lesson, but how much depends very much upon the conditions — upon the time at the disposal of the teacher, the class of students he is dealing with and the importance of the lesson. In approaching an important lesson, deserving of a great deal of consideration, when the time at my disposal was limited, I have often felt as Mr. Depew says he did in his college days when the sententious professor of elocution said to him, 'Sir, your time is three minutes, and your subject, The Immortality of the Soul.' . . .

"A great mistake commonly made by young teachers is that of explaining too much — of being too anxious to help the student instead of making him help himself. The word education is derived from *e, out,* and *ducere, lead,* a leading out. The great art in teaching is to draw out the student, as he advances in the study. The teacher must explain the important rules and principles and emphasize their importance, but he should try to get the student to work out the problems for himself as much as possible."

Cultivate simplicity of statement. The power of stating a thing in language so simple, clear and direct as to be understood by the dullest student in the class is a great art.

In teaching there is a temptation to elaborate, to be expansive. Train yourself to shun it relentlessly. A writer in one of the professional papers says:

> Commercial teachers usually talk too much. They do too much for the student and communicate to him what he should get from his own observation and deliberation. A boy so trained will go into a business office and expect the proprietor to follow the same practice, but the proprietor does not do that, and consequently the boy is lost. A very important part of his training has been neglected. If I were to be asked for what I consider the most important habit a teacher should cultivate I should say, "Do not talk too much. Speak only when it is necessary. If you can, direct a student how to find out for himself what he requires. Give him a simple direction and let him do the rest himself." An enthusiastic teacher becomes so thoroughly saturated with his work that

it is very natural for him to overdo the matter of instruction. From what I say it must not be inferred that I mean he should become so silent that he ceases to be an instructor. That is the other extreme. He should exercise a fine discriminating judgment in saying just the right word at the right time.

If an unfortunate reader of this article, who is a teacher, will on the following day take himself in hand in the schoolroom, and endeavor to condense into the fewest possible words the instruction he gives to his students, he will be astonished in a very short time at the great saving in his physical strength and the greater self-reliance and application which will shortly be observed in his students.

Now, brevity in speech must not be understood to mean surliness, curtness or sarcasm. These are three weapons that come easy to the teacher, but which are boomerangs that return to the teacher and do far more harm than good. Sarcasm in the schoolroom is a splendid disciplinary agent, but it must be exercised with the utmost caution; curtness and surliness are never permissible.

No instruction is valuable which depends upon arbitrary practice or application without an understanding of the reason for the thing that is being applied. Therefore make it a practice to explain the *reason* for each rule or principle before the illustrations are practiced. With the fundamental rules, it is usually sufficient to explain that they represent the *natural way* of writing the forms.

Another important feature in presentation that I wish to comment on is this: Make your students feel that they can "get" the lesson from your explanations if they will give their undivided attention. Caution them against putting off "getting" the lesson until they are alone in their private study. Private study should be used only to augment and deepen the impression of what you have said. It is well to bear in mind the dictum of Herbert Spencer, "To give the net product of the inquiry without the inquiry that leads to it is both enervating and inefficient."

We come now to the second process —

THE APPLICATION

Having explained a rule clearly and briefly, direct the students to practice the illustrations which you have placed on the board.

Be *explicit* in your directions — "You will now write (so many) lines of these words, making the forms slowly and carefully." It is important to have a *well-defined plan of practice*, which should be clearly stated and rigidly enforced until it becomes a matter of routine. Assign so many lines of each shorthand form to be written by the student, with about so many forms to the line. The last mentioned direction is for the purpose of preventing the students filling up the lines with a few, large, sprawling outlines.

As they practice the forms, pass around and examine their work. The knowledge that you are watching them, and are interested in what they are doing, will develop a desire to excel — to merit your approbation — and this spirit of emulation is productive of the best results.

When you think it necessary, you may criticize and correct the outlines; but great tact should be exercised in doing this, especially during the first week or two. Find something to praise — the size of the characters, or some curve or joining, and then say, "But this form might be written a little better, like this —." An experienced teacher says: "Do not emphasize too strongly *criticisms* of pupils' errors. Do not overlook errors, but give more attention to, and say more in *commendation* of, what the student has done correctly. If the student is judiciously praised for everything that he writes correctly, the little that may be necessary to say about his errors is not likely to discourage him." *Praise first — criticize afterwards.*

Do not expect too much precision of form at first; and above all things avoid being hypercritical or "fussy." When the student has gained control of his hand and has a little more familiarity with the forms, you will have plenty of opportunity to enforce exactness of form, and your explanations will then be better understood and become more effective.

It often requires considerable self-control on the part of the teacher to refrain from interrupting students with many explanations and criticisms.

The student should clearly understand from the outset that shorthand is a study requiring much practice, and that he — not you — is to do that practice. *Start him right!* If you begin by explaining everything, correcting everything, giving him constant attention, he will expect you to continue to do so throughout the course, and will feel neglected and helpless when you are not at his elbow. Encourage him to acquire self-reliance, but let him know that you are always ready and willing to assist him when assistance is absolutely necessary.

For his own sake let him understand clearly from the *first* lesson that proficiency in shorthand is attained only by much repetition practice — by writing the outlines over and over again.

This can be conveyed to him as much by the way you act during the first lesson as by stating it in words. If a student stops writing during the practice work, you can step towards him and ask in a solicitous tone, "What is the matter, Mr. Smith?" and then in a kindly but nevertheless authoritative way direct him to continue the practice of the forms until you tell him to stop.

The others will hear what you say and thus the *right idea* will be established at the very beginning. Do not permit any other idea to take root in subsequent lessons; let him understand that nothing will take the place of genuine effort on his part.

In passing around you may notice that several students have a common fault in writing an outline — it may be the joining of a circle or the slant of the curves. Step in front of the class and say: "Let me have your attention for a moment, please. I notice that in writing so-and-so some of you write it like this" (illustrating). Then explain the correct way of making the outline, and have them drill on it.

In doing this it may be necessary to contrast the correct and incorrect forms, but the *faulty forms should not be allowed to remain on the board;* let the emphasis rest strongly on the correct forms. If emphasized too much, a *bad habit* may leave an impression that will lead to unconscious imitation or repetition of it.

For this reason the forms placed on the board should be as graceful and accurate as it is possible for the teacher to make them with freedom of movement. The conscientious teacher will practice diligently to acquire a good *blackboard* style of writing. Students are naturally imitative and pick up almost unconsciously the style of writing placed before them by the teacher.

Explain *one* point at a time; then enforce it by giving the students illustrations for practice. That distinguished educator, Dr. Charles W. Eliot, Ex-President of Harvard University, says:

The next thing education should attend to is the imparting of the habit of *quick and concentrated attention*. Without this there can be no true economy of time. A prolonged attention is not natural to children, and should not be demanded of them, but quick and concentrated attention may be reasonably expected for brief intervals from every child. As the age increases, the possible period of close attention will grow longer and longer.

We all recognize the truth of this statement, and it is well to keep it steadily in mind in all our classroom work. As you can secure from your students quick and concentrated attention for a brief period only, talk briefly, interestingly, explain one point at a time — just one point — and enforce that point by earnest practice.

From motives of economy many schools supply students with cheap notebooks and pencils, and sometimes students buy such notebooks and pencils at the stores. Nothing can be more detrimental to the progress of the shorthand student than poor materials. A well-known reporter says: "When I see some of the notebooks and pencils used by stenographers, I sometimes wonder how these stenographers manage to write. No mechanic could use poor tools in his work, and produce good, fast work. Artists and experts are not satisfied with anything but the finest tools and instruments. The stenographer should have the same spirit. The cost of the best is only a trifle more, and the better and finer work done often results in a reduced size of writing which makes the best material the cheapest after all."

There is a lack of uniformity and orderliness in having various kinds of notebooks. Just as an orderly, well-kept office inspires the office force to be neat and orderly, so good notebooks and pencils inspire the student to do good work. Therefore see that your students have good notebooks and good pencils, and that they keep the pencils sharp, which will aid them in making neat, clean-cut outlines and insure a light touch.

Let us now consider the third process —

THE EXAMINATION

No part of the work is more important than tests and examinations to determine the student's knowledge of the principles of shorthand as he progresses, and perhaps no portion of the work is more neglected. It is in the examination that the intelligence, tact, industry, and teaching qualities of the teacher are brought out unmistakably. Show me a teacher's methods of testing students, grading papers, and system of promotion, and I will tell you the quality of his work — and the success he reaches in preparing stenographers for the exacting demands of modern business.

I hasten to assure you, however, that I shall not prescribe a method of performing this part of the work except to make some suggestions based upon experience. Although I have been teaching shorthand for a quarter of a century, I am free to confess that I have not by any means discovered the ideal method of giving examinations. There are, however, some general propositions which now meet with almost universal acceptance, at least as far as teachers of Gregg Shorthand are concerned. These are:

1. That in shorthand it is necessary to insist upon a certain standard of accuracy of *form* as well as in the application of the rules.

2. That a *practical understanding of the application of a rule* is vastly more important than a knowledge of the exact wording of it.

3. That an understanding of the practical application of a rule is best ascertained by requiring the student to write words illustrating the rule that are not given in the lesson.

4. That new words and new sentences arouse the interest of the student, and develop his constructive

power, and consequently his ability to deal more promptly with new words.

A few comments on tests and examinations, as a whole, may be of service. There is a wide divergence of opinion as to the benefits of examinations. Some distinguished educators are opposed to examinations, but mainly on the ground that they interfere with continuous work, and for this reason I believe that the tests should be short, such as may be given in one period, so that they may not interfere with the onward progress of the student.

Properly conducted, examinations give students an opportunity to discover for themselves many of their weak points, and perhaps therein lies their greatest value. The examination is of much more benefit to the student than to the teacher. The teacher generally knows the student's capabilities. The examination serves also as a review, and brings all the work he has done into a comprehensive view, and is therefore of great value. The student should be induced to feel that the examination is but another form of recitation — that his actual knowledge of the subject is not affected by disclosing his weaknesses.

Preparation should be made for the regular periodical examination by giving frequent tests on words under the principles contained in certain groups of lessons. These tests not only strengthen knowledge of the principles, but tend to relieve the student of the nervousness that is often present on examination day. *Progressive Exercises,* and the supplementary exercises given each year in the *Gregg Writer,* serve admirably for tests on the lessons. In both tests and examinations I think great care should be exercised to avoid selecting words that involve too intricate word-building. It is very easy to err on the side of making the words so difficult as to discourage the student.

The younger and more inexperienced students, too, often have difficulty in writing the correct forms — especially in the advanced work — not so much because they are *unable to apply the principles of shorthand*, as on account of unfamiliarity with the words and their pronunciation. In shorthand, as in spelling, there are many words that may be called "catch" words, and these should be avoided in examinations. Such words may be used as a special drill in regular recitation.

In closing, let me say a word or two of the value of *personality* in getting results. A keen sympathy with the aims and ambitions of the students is one of the quickest means of getting into that close personal relationship which is so necessary for both student and teacher in the development of the student's abilities. This can best be attained by letting the student feel that you are a *leader* and *guide* and not a *critic*. Too many teachers, especially the younger and inexperienced, are apt to feel that they are not fulfilling their mission unless they put themselves in the attitude of critics. There can be no greater mistake. You at once antagonize the student, and all that confidence and freedom of expression, and that unfolding of his real self are lost to you — you never get at his better side, the side which will lead both him and you to success. If the student feels that you are his *guide and friend*, and that he can come to you in the fullest confidence, without fear of criticism, when he meets a difficult situation, you have done more for the development of that student than you could by all the criticisms you could ever make. On the other hand, there is such a thing as being too much of a guide — the student will *lean* on you instead of being self-reliant. The quality of self-reliance must be cultivated. He must learn that while you may plaster his pathway all along with signposts for his guidance, he must do the traveling for himself—that nothing can ever be substituted for his own energy, industry, intelligence, and initiative.

THE ART OF TEACHING SHORTHAND

Read before the
Central Commercial Teachers'
Association, Omaha, Nebr.
May, 1905

THE ART OF TEACHING SHORTHAND

THE "Art of Teaching Shorthand" is such a broad subject that I shall not attempt to do more in this paper than to give some thoughts bearing on certain phases of it which have occurred to me in my experience. I can do no more, perhaps, than open a discussion which will lead us into viewing some of the problems from different angles. If I do this much, I shall be satisfied.

As the business man of to-day has been educated to demand a higher standard of efficiency in his stenographic force than formerly, there must be a corresponding advance in the methods of teaching shorthand and typewriting if we would meet these requirements. The demand for speed in execution has grown in the profession of shorthand as in everything else. Work of all kinds is now done under greater pressure than ever before.

The keen competition between commercial schools seems to render it impracticable to lengthen the course of instruction materially, and yet the teacher of to-day is expected to produce *much better equipped* stenographers and typewriter operators than formerly, not only from the standpoint of technical skill, but of a wider cultural education. This additional cultural work can be done effectively in the high school by the lengthening of the course, but the commercial school must produce results in a shorter time. It is necessary, therefore, for the teacher in the commercial school to intensify his instruction. While it is safe to say that the time devoted to the subjects included in a shorthand course has not been increased to any appreciable extent in the business school, there has been in the past ten years a demand by business men of fully twenty-five per cent increase in efficiency, which means that the students must accomplish just that much more in the time that custom has established as necessary to prepare for stenographic work.

This being the case, it is obvious that improved methods of instruction are imperatively demanded to meet present-day conditions.

And while this demand for increased efficiency has been growing and is still growing at a tremendous rate, there can be no change in the fundamental processes of writing shorthand — processes that are entirely distinct from any improvement in the shorthand systems themselves — and must ever be present, whatever the shorthand system used. Let us consider briefly what these processes are, and we shall realize how great are the problems involved in teaching shorthand, as well as in acquiring sufficient skill in writing to meet existing requirements. A keen analytical writer on this subject has said:

There are at least five distinct mental operations carried on continuously during verbatim reporting. First, there is the sensation of sound received by the ear. Second, there is the perception by the brain of the word uttered — practically simultaneously with the sensation of a hearing in the case of a distinct speaker, but often delayed a large fraction of a second when a speaker drops his voice, or a witness in court has a foreign accent. In the third place, the stenographer must analyze the structure of all the less common words in the sentences, all except the stock words or phrases, which he writes by a practically automatic habit. Fourth, these relatively uncommon words must be put on paper according to the principles of the system employed. This one operation involves many subordinate and infinitely swift efforts of recollection, association, and decision. Fifth, all these mental operations are carried on while the pen or pencil is from two or three words to an entire sentence behind the speaker — this of course in rapid speaking — thereby complicating the situation by compelling memory to keep pace with attention. In other words, while the scribe is writing the predicate of one sentence and analyzing an unfamiliar word in the subject of the next, he is at the same time giving his auditory attention to the predicate of the second sentence then being uttered by the speaker. This is impossible to an untrained mind. The average educated person cannot retain more than perhaps six or eight words of the exact phraseology of a speaker at one time. The competent stenographer can hold ten, fifteen, twenty words, or even more in his memory, while at the same time taxing his mind by the act of writing the words that preceded.

The truth of what this writer says is obvious to us all and there is forced upon us at once the conclusion that the teaching of shorthand presents some peculiar and distinctive problems in pedagogy. I say "peculiar and distinctive" because the ordinary principles of pedagogy cannot always be applied in shorthand instruction, because it is an entirely distinctive problem.

The teaching of bookkeeping is largely a mental problem; the teaching of penmanship is largely a manual one. The teaching of shorthand combines both problems — and in a combination that is complex in the highest degree.

In teaching bookkeeping it is not of great importance that the work be done quickly. Speed here, as elsewhere, is desirable; but it *is* of the greatest importance that it be done *accurately*. One of our problems is the thorough correlation of these two phases of shorthand work — that is, of acquiring *both* speed and accuracy.

Let me draw your attention for a moment to the last named condition of which the writer just quoted speaks, namely — the training of the memory, and the development of concentration, to enable the student to remember as many words as possible while recording other words. Memory training and complete concentration, to my mind, present a distinctive factor in the teaching of shorthand — memorizing not in the sense of storing up in the mind facts or information for future use, but temporarily holding suspended the exact words of a speaker, given perhaps very rapidly, until they can be written, to be then forgotten.

This training must necessarily be a part of the course in the training of all shorthand students and, until the ability to retain a large number of words is developed, a high degree of skill cannot be attained; and this factor, as has been said before, is quite distinct from the *mastery of the principles* of shorthand, and is not affected by the *system* which is being studied. It is this faculty that gives the expert shorthand writer the ability to make the process of writing *continuous*. It *may* be possible to simplify the principles of shorthand construction, so that the mind may construct the word forms more easily, and it *may* be possible to render the joinings and characters more easy and natural, so as to lessen the manual labor in executing them, as has been done in modern systems, but it is not possible in a few hours to endow the student with the trained memory which will permit of the performance of the complex mental and manual acts required in very rapid shorthand writing.

How can we in the schoolroom give this memory training effectively in a course that is already burdensomely heavy? One of the ablest teachers we have ever had in the profession, Mr. J. Clifford Kennedy, it seems to me, has made a very valuable suggestion. He made it a practice to give one dictation each day for the purpose of training the students to remember a series of words. He would dictate from ten to fifteen words and the students would not write until he had uttered the last word — which he indicated by tapping his desk. They would then begin to write, and when they had finished he would dictate another line or two while they refrained from writing until he again tapped the desk, and so on. His method was effective. I have used it myself, and it is surprising the attention value it has, and the interest it lends to the work of dictation.

A well-known reporter, Mr. W. E. McDermut, in a recent paper, said: "In David Wolfe Brown's book on *Factors of Shorthand Speed* he refers to what he calls the 'word-carrying faculty,' the ability to carry a number of words in the mind while catching up. The faculty may be improved by keeping a safe distance behind the dictator while going at a moderate speed, and gradually increasing the distance that the writer can keep behind, as well as the speed. . . . In dictating to classes a good beginning in this way can be made by dictating short questions and answers, the student not to begin writing the question until the dictation of the answer is begun, and so on."

And while on the subject of memory training, there is another act which must be given attention — *hearing*. The ear must be trained to catch and *digest* words.

Let us return to the acts involved in shorthand writing — for I have not mentioned all of them. While the writer of shorthand is hearing, thinking out, remembering and recording the words of the speaker or dictator, he has other work to do. He must turn the pages of his notebook from time to time, make corrections occasionally, observe proportion in writing the characters — all operations necessitating a share of the attention. If he is to make an intelligent report, he must pay close attention to the purport of the speaker's remarks. This last phase of the work is of the highest importance in making an intelligent transcript, being almost impossible if the writer is unable to comprehend the meaning of what the speaker is saying.

It has been said that the practice of shorthand brings into active, instantaneous operation all the faculties of the mind, and that the attainment of a high degree of skill in shorthand writing is equivalent to a proportionate increase in mental activity.

From this partial statement of what is done in actual shorthand writing, it will be clear that the teaching of the subject has distinctive problems, and affords the teacher exceptional opportunities for diversified methods.

How shall we develop speed with

accuracy in the shortest possible time? In other words, how shall we prepare our students to become efficient stenographers and at the same time give them that correct fundamental training which shall enable them to develop a high degree of skill?

It is my opinion that in the past we have laid too great stress upon *accuracy*, and paid too little attention to the development of speed from a scientific point of view. It is a common fallacy that "speed will come with practice."

Without in the least depreciating the importance of accuracy, I believe that we have insisted too much upon accuracy without regard to speed, and by so doing have fastened upon our students a sluggish method of forming the characters from which, in many cases, they have been unable to free themselves in after years. I am firmly of the belief that *speed in execution should be developed along with a theoretical knowl-*

edge of the principles, and not postponed until the writer has mastered the principles.

I have heard teachers, in speaking about this matter, say, "Oh, well, the students will learn the knack of speed in actual work outside the school." That view of the matter is a survival of the old idea, now fast dying out. Accuracy and speed can be combined from the very beginning, and should be. Who can say that the steps of a runner are any less accurate than are those of the walker? The secret of speed in execution lies largely in getting the right idea.

It has long seemed to me a strange anomaly in business education that the value of movement exercises should be so universally recognized in the teaching of penmanship, and that such exercises should be almost entirely ignored in teaching shorthand. The technique of shorthand writing is of the utmost importance, and yet most of us, I am afraid, lay the stress on "principles" and not "practice."

If it be conceded that movement drills in penmanship develop a more perfect command of hand and pen, it would seem to follow that they are absolutely indispensable in teaching shorthand, where rapid and accurate execution simply cannot be dispensed with.

The explanation of this apparent inconsistency may possibly be found in the belief that shorthand, requiring as it does greater nicety of execution, is liable under free movement exercises to develop into an illegible scrawl. While this may be true to some extent with the student who has not been properly trained in the beginning, I believe that an injustice is done to the careful and conscientious student by the utter neglect of such drills. A recognition of the fact that a greater nicety of execution is demanded for shorthand writing in order to gain speed in writing and the legibility necessary for rapid, accurate transcription, would seem to emphasize the absolute necessity for movement drills to develop manual skill.

We can't get away from the fact that rapid shorthand writing is largely a matter of *manual* skill. Shorthand writing is *writing*, not drawing. This fact must become a fixture in the mind of the student from the first day of his work, and it must be doubly impressed that all that is written must be read. I am not one who believes that the shorthand characters must be drawn with mathematical accuracy in the early lessons. I think the characters must be correct, and held as nearly as possible to the ideal, but they must be *written* so, not drawn.

Many teachers are a little too "textbooky," if I may so express it. They use modern text-books written from the teacher's point of view; they know these books from cover to cover, and they teach the principles much more thoroughly than the teacher of the old school; but when they have done all that, they are apt to think that the development of speed lies entirely with the student, and that all he needs is continuous dictation practice. They feel that they have done their part in teaching rules and form, and the rest lies with the student and his employer.

Willing and anxious as they are to assist the student at all stages of the work, they have no systematic plan for giving him an insight into the peculiar knack of rapid writing or of training him in those time-saving expedients and modifications of form which *must* be acquired before a high degree of skill can be attained.

In my opinion the shorthand teacher

owes it to the reputation of the school with which he is connected to demonstrate to the students that under his instruction they acquire something outside the text-book — something that cannot be acquired by any amount of home study or mere dictation practice.

One of the most powerful aids in imparting to others the knack of writing shorthand *rapidly* is the ability to write rapidly and to demonstrate how it is done. Not rapidity in the sense that the teacher must be a "record breaker," or a "speedist," but he ought to have sufficient executional skill to show students that he is a capable writer himself. And it may be remarked in passing that the teacher who takes the trouble to acquire this skill will have revealed to him some of the things behind the scenes which will do more to help him to secure results than anything he has ever undertaken.

It is not sufficient to give general suggestions from time to time, for such academic instruction, however valuable it may be, leaves only a transient impression on the mind of the average student and is of little practical value in the development of speed.

To be of any effective service, the instruction must be supplemented by regular and intense application under the eye of the teacher. I advocate a systematic course of exercises for advanced students, mapped out with the same care as are the drills now used in teaching penmanship or touch typewriting.

Such drills will result in a great improvement in the style of writing, and will have the effect of keeping steadily before the student the importance of facility of execution. In an article sometime ago in the *American Penman,* Mr. Carl C. Marshall, in speaking of a visit to a penmanship class conducted by

Mr. F. B. Courtney, said: "I noticed that the class did not follow the count uniformly, that is, did not 'write together' or in the same time. I afterwards called Mr. Courtney's attention to this and asked him if it was intended that they should do so. 'Oh, no,' he said, 'the purpose of the count is primarily to secure speed, not uniformity of movement, which is not only impracticable but not really desirable. I think the counting helps them to avoid the drawing habit or the construction of the letters slowly and without regard to the time. It keeps the paramount idea of speed constantly before them.'" Mr. Marshall adds, "This was the first time that the psychological value of the counting device had been made plain to me." So it is with shorthand penmanship drills when conducted with snap and vim. They eliminate the "drawing habit" and keep the "paramount idea of speed" constantly before the students.

The advantages of the shorthand penmanship drill may be briefly summed up as follows:

It relieves the monotony of ordinary routine dictation and by keeping the student interested in his work insures more certain and rapid progress.

It promotes harmony between the mental and physical actions in shorthand writing, the hand being trained to respond more promptly to the thought transmitted to it from the brain.

It leads the student to study the individual peculiarities of his writing, and by familiarizing him with the modifications which outlines undergo when rapidly written, enables him to acquire greater fluency in reading.

It teaches him to control the unnecessary movements of the hand and to acquire knowledge in this direction, which might otherwise come to him only after years of actual work.

It compels a student who has a sluggish or awkward method of writing to realize by comparison that the fault is with himself, and not with the teacher or the system he writes.

It trains him to make rapid transitions between words, to move easily and rapidly from the end of one line to the beginning of the next, and from page to page.

It gives him a swiftness of action that is carried into all the other writing.

It shortens the time required to attain proficiency in shorthand, and thus allows more time to be given to typewriting, spelling, punctuation, etc.

It promotes a spirit of emulation and inspires the student with greater confidence in his teacher.

It is of the highest importance to maintain the interest of the student in his work. There is too much routine and too much continuous dictation in our classrooms. Continuous dictation acts as a soporific, and the evidence of this will be found in the large percentage of students who find it necessary to support their heads with their hands while taking dictation.

The penmanship and other exercises that I have suggested will impart an interest and a vim to the work in the classroom which will induce students to do their very best, and this quite apart from the value of the exercises in developing combined speed and accuracy. The former superintendent of the Chicago schools, Mr. Cooley, in reply to a criticism about the introduction of fads into the public schools, said: "The fads are essential. It is impossible to keep a child's attention at a set task for very long. They have their three R's and then their games, cooking, sewing, etc., and then they go back to the first. In this way the children enjoy all the studies."

Now as our students are but children of a larger growth, what Mr. Cooley says applies to our work. We should make it more interesting, more intense.

"TRICKS OF THE TRADE" IN TEACHING SHORTHAND

Read before the National Shorthand Teachers' Association St. Louis, Missouri, 1901

"TRICKS OF THE TRADE" IN TEACHING SHORTHAND

THE title of my paper was suggested by the concluding remark of a school proprietor who applied to me for a teacher. After mentioning the requirements, he said: "To sum it all up, I want a man who is thoroughly qualified — one who knows all the tricks of the trade." At first, I was inclined to resent the imputation that there were any tricks in our trade, but subsequent reflection and observation have convinced me that we cannot, with truth, say "there are tricks in all trades but ours."

WHAT "TRICKS OF THE TRADE" MEANS

The phrase is not used in a derogatory sense; in our profession it is usually intended to convey the idea of adaptability, tact, experience, etc. In every line of human endeavor, the man who is valuable to his employer is the man who knows the tricks of his trade. It is just as true in our profession as it is of the shoe clerk who sells you a pair of shoes for seven dollars when you intended to purchase a pair for half that amount on entering the store. And by that it is not meant the man who is familiar with all the sharp practices and underhanded tricks of a trade, but the man who makes friends because of his knowledge of his business and of human nature, and who, by his industry, foresight, and adaptability to different personalities, is able to make the best use of his knowledge. Such is the man who is familiar with the legitimate "tricks" of his trade. It is he who reaches the highest success in any line, whose force is felt not only in his own particular profession, but carries the influence of his forcefulness into all branches of human activity. But, back of this familiarity with human nature, there must be a wider and deeper knowledge — knowledge of the thousands of details, small in themselves, but which go to make up the whole. It is the faculty for going into the very heart of a thing and studying it analytically, the faculty that enables a Kipling to write with equally profound knowledge of the freaks of a locomotive, or still greater freaks of human sentiment; that enables a J. Pierpont Morgan to so arrange his forces as to bring about financial combinations that are staggering in their magnitude; that enables a Marconi to send electric impulses across the sea by methods hitherto undreamt of.

The shorthand teacher usually has but little to do with the business management of the school with which he is associated; but whether he has any word in the business management or not, he can make himself of more value to his employer by familiarizing himself with all the phases of the school management, in order that he may be able to understand the school's policy and become an effective factor in its success.

MASTERY OF THE SUBJECT

First of all, it goes without saying, he should be master of the theory and technique of the art which he teaches. This is an indispensable trick. Nothing carries conviction so quickly, or is the source of greater inspiration to his students, than evidence that the teacher can do what he teaches.

The teacher who gives a practical demonstration of his ability to perform the feats which he asks of his pupils, has done more perhaps to gain the confidence of his students than he could by any other means. There is such a wide difference between the theory of any art and the application of the theory to practical work that it seems to me this is a point that should receive a great deal of earnest attention from the teacher. Methods of execution in writing can only be taught by practical illustration. One may have an almost perfect conception of how a thing should be done, and yet not be able to do it until he has seen it done. Such knowledge does not come from a mere conception that this or that thing can be done; it comes only after infinitely patient toil.

But, in illustrating a point, the teacher should not allow his own expertness in execution to become so apparent as to discourage his students. He should endeavor to keep his execution within the bounds of the capacity of his students; it should be an illustration of the methods of movements rather than a demonstration of the speed at which such movements may be made, otherwise the effect may be opposite from that which he desires. If he can create the impression upon the students that it is all very simple, and that by a little extra effort they can do as well, he will unconsciously develop in them a feeling of power that will have the most beneficial effect.

RESOURCEFULNESS NECESSARY AT TIMES

While all this is true, it sometimes happens that through circumstances a teacher is thrown into new surroundings and finds himself in a position where his only salvation is his ingenuity and ability to adapt himself to the new conditions. In such circumstances, I believe it is perfectly justifiable to take advantage of whatever tricks he may be able to devise in order to carry out his work successfully. To illustrate:

I recently visited a school where the

teacher had been obliged to make a change of systems a few weeks previously. As I entered the classroom he was placing a shorthand exercise on the board for transcription. He held the text-book in his hand, and appeared to be composing the exercise as he wrote. I was very much impressed with the ease with which he executed the outlines, considering the time he had devoted to the system he was using. The only pauses appeared to be those caused by hesitancy in composing the sentences, but which were in reality caused by his efforts to grasp fully the import of the outlines. Upon investigation, I found that he had collected exercises bearing on each lesson from another teacher and pasted them in his book following the lessons. This man possessed resourcefulness, and to my mind he was perfectly justified in employing such an expedient. His previous experience made him capable of imparting instruction; the fact that he realized his somewhat imperfect knowledge of the instrument he was using, aroused him to use all his resourcefulness to make his instruction effective, and that it was effective was attested by the interest and confidence of his students. If the teacher had not used this "trick," his students would very quickly have detected his weakness, lost confidence in his ability, and become discouraged.

PERSONAL INTEREST IN STUDENTS

A very important point is for the teacher to take a personal interest in the progress of each student, but this must be done without creating any suspicion of partiality. Only by a constant study of the peculiarities of each student, in order that he may give him such encouragement as he needs and point out tactfully the errors of his ways in such a manner as not to antagonize him, can the teacher hope to attain this end. The element of personal interest in his students is a potent one in influencing the success of the teacher as well as that of the student. It is a "trick" that can be acquired only by painstaking care, and requires the exercise of rare discrimination, self-control, and a strong sense of justice. It is an art that should be cultivated assiduously. The school proprietor can get students to the school. The success of the student is then practically in the teacher's hands, and the fitness of the teacher for the position which he holds will depend upon how well the pupil accomplishes his task. The teacher should bring every influence to bear to make the progress of the student so sure and thorough that when he leaves, whether it be in six months or a year, he will be qualified to discharge his duties creditably to himself and to the institution where he received his training. While the teacher is employed primarily to "teach," there is much more to be taught than the mere art of shorthand writing. He should make a study of the defects in the training of his students, and try as far as possible to correct them. Anything that would tend to lessen the student's chances for success, such as lack of taste in dress, untidiness, peculiar mannerisms, etc., may be corrected by occasional general talks on such subjects, and in extreme cases by tactful confidential talks. It is manifestly impossible for teachers handling large classes to remember the name of each student at all times — although it will be surprising to those who have not tried it how quickly the faculty can be acquired—but it is a habit that the teacher should acquire as early in his experience as possible. There is hardly anything more displeasing to the student than for his teacher to neglect to address him by name.

SECURING THE ATTENTION OF STUDENTS

The art of holding the attention of the student while presenting the lesson; of repeating the explanations, if need be, in different language, until they have been thoroughly impressed on the mind of the student, is a subject that will require much earnest study on the part of the teacher.

At this point the teacher will have full opportunity to exercise whatever ingenuity and resourcefulness he may possess, because methods of presentation that would appeal quickly and effectively to one class of students, might have exactly the opposite effect on others. The teacher should make a careful study of the personnel of his classes, and adopt methods that will comprehend the various mental capabilities of his students, if possible. A mistake many inexperienced teachers make is to adapt their methods to a few of the bright pupils of one class, to the utter confusion of the less intellectual students.

THE TEACHER SHOULD BE SUPERIOR TO THE TEXT-BOOK

Another point at which many teachers fail is in making their own instruction subordinate to that of the text-book. The difference between such instruction and real instruction is just the difference that distinguishes the written play from the acted play. In the former the whole mass of words is lifeless, except to the highly imaginative; in the latter art, environment, and the living words of the actors make a lasting impression.

THE USE OF THE BLACKBOARD

Perhaps nothing marks the difference between the experienced teacher and the novice more than the method of using the blackboard, and I would name the intelligent use of the blackboard as one of the greatest tricks in our trade. From the position that he assumes before the board, the inexperienced teacher often appears to believe that his pupils can see through him, I mean in the literal sense. But in our profession the art of "side-stepping" is just as important as it is in the noble art of self-defense. The experienced teacher after writing the outlines on the board will step aside in an easy, natural manner so that students in all parts of the room may have a clear view of the board. The young teacher is very apt to write his outlines so small and faint that they cannot be seen by any except those who are close at hand. The knack of retaining proportion of outline while writing large on the board is a trick that requires considerable practice.

KEEPING "JUST AHEAD" OF STUDENTS

The inexperienced teacher is frequently inclined to "show off" by writing very rapidly on the board, to the utter bewilderment of his students. This may impress them with a due appreciation of his ability as a writer of shorthand, but it has a most discouraging effect on the student who contrasts his snail-like execution with that of the teacher. On the other hand, the teacher who has, through long training and experience, mastered the method of handling blackboard work, will write just a little ahead of his pupils — enough to make them feel that with a little effort they could do as well — but he will always be *just ahead* of his pupils.

GENIALITY — AND DISCIPLINE

The teacher should possess a genial and amiable disposition, but he should not allow the discipline of his room to become lax in his efforts to be good natured, nor should he allow students to get the idea that the acquisition of a business education is anything but a serious matter. He should glow with such a warmth of good-will as to be a constant incentive to his students to emulate his example. He must put vim and enthusiasm into his work; all his acts must be so businesslike that his students will unconsciously acquire the habit. He must cultivate his memory so that he will be relentless in getting the work he requires of his students. He should be very careful, however, in deciding upon a policy, to be sure that he can carry it out. Work started by a teacher, and afterwards abandoned, will create a feeling of distrust in his ability.

A moderate amount of work thoroughly accomplished each day will be far more effective than a large amount imperfectly gone over. Students are very quick to detect imperfections in a teacher's character, and weak points in his methods, and he must therefore constantly strive to make his work as strong as possible. The teacher should impress upon his pupils the advantage of thorough preparation, and show them the folly of leaving school before they are competent to fill the best positions. I believe that the teacher in advocating a long course is rendering the student the greatest possible service, as well as doing his full duty by his employers and to the commercial community. Business men nowadays make such exacting requirements of stenographers that it is imperative that the school expecting to keep in the front rank should so qualify its students that they can enter upon their duties without having to go through a long course of "breaking in."

It will require rare judgment on the

part of the teacher to effect this result without creating the suspicion that he is working solely for his employer's interests.

KEEPING UP-TO-DATE

The wide-awake teacher will keep fully alive to the methods pursued by business houses in the handling of correspondence. Methods change constantly, and the teacher who would attain the great success, and enlarge his influence in his profession, must keep up-to-date in his methods. He can do this by keeping in close touch with his former students who have gone out into the business world, and by reading the shorthand magazines. And while he is making a study of these methods, he should not forget the hundreds of ambitious teachers who, perhaps, may not be so fortunately situated for studying methods, and give them the benefit of his experience through this Association and the shorthand magazines.

DIFFERENCES IN SCHOOL CONDITIONS

It has often occurred to me that in all the meetings of this Association which I have attended, there has never been any reference made to the differences existing between the methods of conducting a day school and a night school in a large city. These are important considerations, and personally I should like to hear them discussed. When I visit a school in a small town, I always envy the shorthand teacher the class of students he has under his charge. They are generally earnest and ambitious, and are willing to devote considerable time to practice outside school hours. The city student, as a rule, is not so thorough in his work, and it is a severe drain upon the teacher's energies to keep him sufficiently interested to perform the work assigned to him.

DAY SCHOOL AND NIGHT SCHOOL

The same difference exists between the day school and the night school in a large city. In the day school the students are usually very young, and as they have no idea of the value of time, it is imperative that the teacher should be constantly on the alert. In the night school the students are older, and as they are employed during the day, they are accustomed to strict discipline and continuous labor. As they have taken up the study of choice, and have not been sent by their parents, they are liable to discontinue the study at any time unless they are kept interested and believe they are making satisfactory progress.

Night school work has always had a fascination for me, perhaps because of my desire to help those who are trying to help themselves. I believe that the methods employed in the night school should differ materially from those of the day school. As the night school students are employed in the business hours, they know a great deal about office routine, business terms and forms, and consequently they require less instruction in these things. They can apply their shorthand and typewriting more readily on that account, but as they are at work all day, it is absolutely essential that they should be kept interested and wide-awake. Less copying work should therefore be assigned to them, and they should be given a great deal more blackboard and dictation work. As they have already acquired businesslike habits of deportment, the teacher can assume toward them a more genial attitude than is possible in the day school. This adaptability to the varying needs of the day and night school is one of the tricks I would require above all others in a teacher in my employ.

THE ELEMENT OF HUMOR

At the convention of this Association last year, we had with us a teacher who was unquestionably a master of his profession, but who has now passed away — Mr. Benjamin Stanley Banks. I believe that his death has been a distinct loss to our profession, and that his place cannot be adequately filled. Recently one of his pupils, who is now in charge of the shorthand department of a large commercial school, told me that Mr. Banks was fully alive to the importance of keeping his students interested in their work by novel methods of instruction. He said that in dictation work he frequently relieved the monotony by the introduction of impromptu talks on various subjects to be reported by the students, and he made it an invariable rule to dictate an extract from Mark Twain, Max Adler, or some other humorist as the last exercise of the day, in order that the students might go away laughing and in good spirits. While this method would not at all times be advisable, it seems to me that a good feeling inspired by such a course, would occasionally be very beneficial in relieving the monotony of a hard day's work.

IMPORTANCE OF WELL-DIRECTED ENERGY

In closing I desire to mention that which in any line of business counts for more, perhaps, with one exception — brains — than any other, and that is, well-directed energy. To a teacher, energy is as indispensable as a mastery of the subject he teaches. A teacher using mediocre or even inferior methods, who backs up his work with snap and energy, will accomplish creditable results where a more brilliant man with less energy would prove a failure. The successful teacher must be able to create an atmosphere of energetic action that will arouse his pupils to put forth their best efforts. But he must learn to judge between apparent energy and actual energy. Nothing is more absurd than a man rushing hither and thither, sputtering and fuming, in the belief that he is accomplishing something. It is the escaping steam that makes the noise. A teacher may possess a vast storehouse of energy and yet fail to accomplish results because of his inability to direct his energy in the proper channels.

The teacher must be the adviser and guardian spirit of his pupil, and it should be his constant care to see that each day marks a distinct step on life's road, and that, above all, the student can never say, "I came out by the same door wherein I entered."

EFFICIENT STENOGRAPHERS
WHAT SHOULD THEIR ATTAINMENTS AND QUALIFICATIONS BE WHEN THEY GRADUATE FROM THE SCHOOL

Read before the New England Business College Association
Woonsocket, Rhode Island
1910

EFFICIENT STENOGRAPHERS

THE word "efficient," as commonly used, is such an elastic term that perhaps Webster's view of it may help us in formulating a standard of comparison in the present discussion. His definition of "efficient" is: "Causing effects; producing results; not inactive, slack or incapable; characterized by energetic and useful activity."

In order to understand fully the conditions which confront the stenographer who would be classed among the "efficient," let us consider for a moment the present-day demands.

DEMAND CONSTANTLY INCREASING

As American business has grown in complexity, under the influence of expansion, from trade of a purely local nature to that of world-wide extent, the demands laid upon stenographers have also increased in complexity, and the efficient stenographer of to-day must include in his equipment far more than was required ten or even five years ago. And it may be mentioned in passing that while expansion of trade was inevitable to a people imbued with the spirit of enterprise as Americans are, yet it has been greatly facilitated and hastened through the instrumentality of modern shorthand and the typewriter. Business men of executive ability and imagination have been able to multiply themselves through the aid of these twin arts, and to handle to-day a volume of business that would have been impossible with the old-time methods.

THE STENOGRAPHER NO LONGER A FAD

Business men were quick to appreciate the value of the stenographer, and have been responsible for his development from a sort of "luxury" or "fad" into one of the most efficient aids in a modern business organization. The stenographer of to-day is not occupied wholly with typing out the letters which the firm sends to the outside world, though of course this comprises a large part of his daily work, but the inter-house correspondence, in which the heads of this business dictate orders and instructions to its various branches, and to its traveling sales force, calls for a technical knowledge of the business that goes far outside the mere business of writing shorthand and typing it on the machine. A large part of these instructions are made up from form books; they require a checking and following up and a collecting of material that lays upon the stenographer duties calling for ability of a different kind from that of merely following orders. As the stenographer's ability to grasp details from a few meager instructions increases, his importance and value to the firm also increases.

THE EFFICIENT STENOGRAPHER ALSO A CORRESPONDENT

The really efficient stenographer in modern business to-day can handle a great deal of the correspondence from a few directions from his employer. He becomes acquainted with the policy of the house, studies his employer's way of handling problems through correspondence, is able to give the personal touch to the firm's correspondence that the head of the firm himself would give. His work becomes truly "characterized by energetic and useful activity." He must be acquainted with the new card records, filing systems, and office practice generally, and this involves a far more intricate knowledge than is commonly supposed.

KEEPING STEP WITH PROGRESS

Recent economic influences have brought about also vast changes in the methods of record keeping and in handling the transactions of business, with which the efficient stenographer must be thoroughly familiar, because they require his services.

Typewriter companies have added new attachments to their machines which make them far more useful, but which also make necessary more knowledge and greater technical skill on the part of the stenographer. Brief as are these references, they give an idea of the complexity of the commercial stenographer's need for special knowledge to enable him to render efficient service.

THE GENERAL STENOGRAPHER

The problem is far more complex and difficult in the case of the general stenographer, who in addition to these qualifications must also have a knowledge of a very wide variety of topics outside, and I might say what would be considered almost foreign to his profession by those not understanding the varied nature of his work. For example, the general stenographer is called upon to do work for the manufacturer, the attorney, the chemist, the physicist, the college professor, the promoter, the physician, the litterateur, the playwright, the mining engineer, and a multitude of other professional men. To perform this service efficiently, he must have a knowledge of the terms and phrases used in these various professions, and his knowledge must be more than superficial.

THE QUALIFICATIONS OF THE BEGINNER

What should the stenographer's attainments and qualifications be when he is graduated from the school? The work of the stenographer is distinctly technical, and therefore in order that his work may produce results, that he may be efficient, the first in importance of his qualifications should be a thorough training in his technical subjects — shorthand, typewriting, and English.

THE IMPORTANCE OF ENGLISH

Before the student of stenography can become really efficient in his technical subjects he must have a solid educational foundation upon which to build. His efficiency as a stenographer is based upon a good working knowledge of the English language. The writer of shorthand merely takes "notes," and does not attempt to take dictation as it appears in print. Necessarily the punctuation, the capitalization, the spelling, the paragraphing, the subheads must be supplied from the stenographer's knowledge of language, and his grasp of the subject; and his efficiency is increased exactly in proportion to the accuracy of his knowledge along these lines. Hence it can be seen that a thorough understanding of grammar and English composition is an indispensable factor in the stenographer's equipment. The student of stenography, however, will find that the work in stenography can be made a great help in learning English.

WORD STUDY

Along with the English, the stenographer must have a thorough training in spelling, and particularly in the *meaning and use of words*. This is generally a weak point in the average stenographer's education — a lack of knowledge of the use of words. To be efficient, the stenographer needs a high school education, and if he has more than this all the better. Naturally such a stenographer can be entrusted with a great deal of the detail work of the correspondence and will be accordingly more valuable.

GENERAL KNOWLEDGE INVALUABLE

He should know commercial arithmetic, commercial law, have a general knowledge of history and of literature, and be a reader of good current literature, in addition to the education already mentioned. In fact, no knowledge that an ordinarily well-educated person possesses can very well be dispensed with in the stenographer's equipment. Since perhaps nine out of ten stenographers are engaged in business, it is evident that the more he knows about business, its methods, its phraseology, the more efficient he becomes.

ACCURACY MORE IMPORTANT THAN SPEED

When we come to the technical subjects of shorthand and typewriting, nothing less than a very high degree of proficiency will meet present-day demands. In shorthand great speed is not so much needed as *accuracy*. A speed of one hundred words a minute on matter of ordinary difficulty is sufficient for the average office position. But the notes taken at this rate should be so legible that the stenographer can utilize his full typewriting speed in transcribing. He cannot be called an efficient stenographer until he can accomplish this. Great stress should therefore be laid upon reading ability.

THE INFLUENCE OF TOUCH TYPEWRITING

The development of typewriting during the last few years has been extraordinary. Since the introduction of touch typewriting both speed and accuracy have been increased in a wonderful degree. An accurate knowledge of what a really capable typewriter operator can accomplish has set the typewriting standard higher every year, and the operator to be really efficient nowadays has to produce a very high class of work. The typewritten page is what the employer *sees;* it must be accurate. He also takes note of time; the typewriting must be done with speed. The operator to fulfill these requirements must stay in school long enough and get the necessary training to meet the new demand. The variety of the typewriter operator's work also is constantly enlarging. He must show skill in every branch of his work. He must be familiar with tabulating devices, the adding machine typewriter, and the various other devices which have recently been added to the machine.

THE INFLUENCE OF LOCAL CONDITIONS

The locality in which the stenographer is to work should also be considered in the problem of efficiency. His knowledge should be adapted to local conditions. For example, the city of Schenectady is an electrical center, and the stenographer working there, of necessity, must be familiar with the terms and phrases used in the electrical industry if he comes in contact with correspondence of this nature. Chicago is a big railroad and packing-house center, requiring a knowledge of these two industries; and in Washington, civil service and governmental terms are common. The stenographer in these places must be familiar with these lines.

PLAIN COMMON SENSE NEEDED

There are various other qualities that need to be emphasized. One of the rarest of qualities among both young men and women entering business is plain common sense. Business is an occupation in which the ability to think, and to put two and two together, is more valuable than any other trait. And yet this ability is the rarest to find. As Elbert Hubbard said:

We are all down on the time book for eight dollars a day, but one reason why some receive less in their pay envelopes is because the cash is held back to pay someone else for looking after them, laying out the work, and holding them to their tasks. I know lots of men who pay seven dollars a day for supervision. The less supervision, the more pay; the more supervision, the less pay.

There should be a new study added to the curriculum of all schools preparing young men and women for business — a study that will develop common sense.

GRADUATION TESTS DELUSIVE

Considerable diversity of opinion exists as to what the graduation test in the technical subjects of a stenographic course should be. Graduation tests at best are delusive. Some of the poorest stenographers I know could pass the average graduation test without the slightest difficulty when it comes to speed in typewriting and in shorthand. The average school holds the student to, say, one hundred words a minute in shorthand and thirty-five words a minute transcribing speed. Generally the matter selected is from business letters, and the ordinary business letter, as we know, is not difficult. A fairer test would be the above figures applied to a newspaper article or an editorial article from a newspaper or magazine, for the reason that the stenographer never knows what line of business he may be engaged in, and his shorthand examination should be on all-round matter which will test his ability to write ordinarily hard *new* matter.

SUMMARY

To sum up the *technical* qualifications the efficient stenographer should have:

1. A thorough knowledge of English — an ability to write a businesslike letter in businesslike English.
2. A knowledge of words which will enable him to substitute the right word when the wrong one is used by his employer.
3. A working knowledge of spelling, punctuation, paragraphing, and good style in arrangement.
4. A shorthand speed of not less than 100 words a minute on ordinarily difficult matter.
5. An ability to read his notes fluently and accurately.
6. A *transcribing* speed of at least thirty-five words a minute in typewriting, and a knowledge of the mechanics and mechanical devices of his machine.
7. A working familiarity with the cultural studies ordinarily included in a commercial high school course.

Of the *general* qualifications the following are indispensable:

1. Common sense.
2. An ambition to give *service* instead of merely to draw salary.
3. The ability to keep the affairs of the business to himself.
4. A desire to climb higher; to make his work merit promotion.
5. Faith in his work and a desire to learn all there is to know about the business.
6. Honesty and loyalty.

When the stenographer possesses all these qualities his work will "cause effects" that will be eminently satisfactory to him and to his employer; his work will be "characterized by energetic and useful activity"; and he can truly call himself an "efficient" stenographer.

THE APPLICATION OF MODERN EFFICIENCY PRINCIPLES TO THE TEACHING OF SHORTHAND

An Address to the "Gregg Shorthand Round Table," at the Eastern Commercial Teachers' Association
April 21, 1916

UNIV.
CALIF.

THE APPLICATION OF MODERN EFFICIENCY PRINCIPLES TO THE TEACHING OF SHORTHAND

IN the brief time allotted to me I cannot do more than outline what I believe to be the next step forward in teaching our special subject. In order to gain your attention I am going to make a bold statement at the very outset. It is this: I believe that the efficiency of most shorthand departments could be increased from twenty-five to fifty per cent by the adoption of the methods I am about to suggest. All I can hope to do within the time limit is to give you a skeleton of the plan, but I hope that what I have to say will be sufficient to induce you to reflect upon it, to investigate, and to experiment with it.

The plan is the application to the teaching of shorthand of what is known in business as scientific management, or efficiency principles. It is well known that the work of many of the great industries and factories has been revolutionized by the work of Frederick Taylor, Frank Gilbreth, Harrington Emerson, and other efficiency engineers. I believe that a similar revolution can be effected in teaching shorthand through the adaptation of efficiency principles to our classroom work.

Let me trace the steps taken by the efficiency engineer in the study of any problem. He first studies the material to be handled by the workmen, and the methods adopted in handling it. Through "motion studies" and "time studies" he sets a standard to be attained, based upon the performance of the best workman. He improves even the performance of the best workman by suggestions based on his observations. He then proceeds to bring all of the workmen up to that standard by the elimination of unnecessary or time-wasting motions in the performance of the work to be done. Let me explain how this was applied to bricklaying.

A LESSON FROM BRICKLAYING

Bricklaying is one of the oldest of trades. Although practiced by millions of men, there has been little or no change in the materials or the manner of doing the work in centuries. An efficiency engineer, Mr. Frank Gilbreth, applied the principles of scientific management to bricklaying with remarkable results. His investigation showed that in laying bricks under standard conditions, the bricklayer made eighteen motions. Applying scientific principles to the problem, Mr. Gilbreth succeeded in reducing the number of motions to five, with the result that the average per man, per hour, which had been 120 bricks, was increased to 350 bricks.

Let us consider what the traditional way of laying bricks is. The bricks are dumped out in a pile, the bricklayer stoops down and picks up a brick out of the pile, examines it, taps it, and if it is a trimmed brick, finds which end should be placed outward, and proceeds to place it in position. Here you have a number of complicated movements. In applying scientific management, Mr. Gilbreth studied the exact position which each of the feet of the bricklayer should occupy with relation to the wall, the mortar box, and the pile of bricks, and so made it unnecessary for him to take a step or two toward the pile of bricks and back again each time a brick was laid. He studied the best height for the mortar box and the brick pile, and then designed a scaffold with a table, upon which all of the materials are placed, so as to keep the bricks, the mortar, the man, and the wall in their proper relative positions. These scaffolds are adjusted for all of the bricklayers as the wall grows in height, by a laborer especially detailed for this purpose. By this means, the bricklayer is saved the effort of stooping down to the level of his feet for each brick and each trowel full of mortar, and then straightening up again. Think of the waste of effort that has gone on through all these years with each bricklayer lowering his body down and raising it again every time a brick, weighing about five pounds, is laid in the wall, and this each bricklayer did about one thousand times a day! The bricks, too, are carefully sorted by a laborer with their best edge on a simple wooden frame, so as to enable him to take hold of each brick in the quickest time and in the most advantageous position. In this way, the bricklayer avoids having to turn the brick over on end to examine it before laying it, and saves, too, the time taken in deciding which is the best edge and end to place upon the outside of the wall. In most cases, he saves the time taken in disentangling the brick from a disorderly pile on the scaffold. We have all seen bricklayers tap each brick several times with the handle of the trowel as it is placed on its bed of mortar so as to secure the right thickness for the joint. Mr. Gilbreth found that by tempering the mortar just right, the bricks could be readily bedded to the proper depth by a downward pressure of the hand with which they were laid.

This will give you an idea of how scientific management is arrived at and applied. It is by intense analysis and study of each movement of the workman and by eliminating one after another all unnecessary movements, and substituting fast for slow movements. It requires very close study of every minute element which in any way affects the speed of the workman.

Another important feature of scientific management is this: that each workman is treated as an individual, and his work is carefully planned for him in advance. He knows just *what* he has to do, and *how much* he has to do per day.

Just as in the traditional method of bricklaying, the increase in the height of a wall being built was dependent upon the slowest workman, so, under the traditional methods of shorthand instruction, the progress of the students is regulated by that of the slowest student in the class. This is true of theory work and it is true of dictation work, which must be governed by the slowest student.

In the study of shorthand, what is the object to be accomplished? It is the recording of words as rapidly as possible. The material, then, with which the student deals is *words;* the tools with which he handles that material are shorthand characters.

The first point, then, to be considered is the nature of the material to be handled — *words.* Unlike bricks, words are not standardized as to size, appearance or frequency of use. A recent monograph issued by the Russell Sage Foundation entitled "A Measuring Scale for Ability in Spelling," by Leonard P. Ayres, states that *ten* words (*the, and, of, to, I, a, in, that, you, for*), with their repetitions, constitute more than one-fourth of all the words we write; and that *fifty* words, with their repetitions, constitute about *one-half* of all the words we write.

Recent investigations of various dictation books made in our own office have shown that more than ninety per cent of all the words used in ordinary dictation are written in accordance with the first ten lessons of our shorthand Manual. It follows from this that much greater attention should be given to these lessons than to the other lessons because exceptional rapidity in doing nine-tenths of the work to be done is of the utmost importance. It has been demonstrated, too, that if a student is drilled systematically and intelligently on the alphabetic characters and combinations in the early lessons, and then given a great variety of actual dictation practice on words, sentences, letters, and articles that may be written in accordance with the principles of these lessons, he is able to handle the less frequent material, the long and uncommon words, with vastly increased facility.

A Lesson from Typewriting

I have given you an illustration of the application of these principles to bricklaying. At this point I should like to direct your attention to the remarkable results that have been secured through the application of these principles to a subject that is closely allied to shorthand — typewriting. You will remember that but a few years ago the championship speed in typewriting was around 80 words a minute; to-day it is about 130 words a minute. It stayed around 80 words a minute until the typewriter companies became interested in the contests as an advertising feature of their machines, and placed experts in charge of the training of their best operators. Then the speed jumped to over 100 words a minute and every year it goes higher, being now far beyond what was believed humanly possible a few years ago.

Take the case of the girl who won the Novice Championship in Typewriting last November. Here was a girl who began the study of typewriting in the regular course at a high school thirteen months before the contest. She made the remarkable record of 114 words a minute, which is far in excess of the championship speeds some years ago. What is more striking about this record is this: that when she went to the office of the typewriter company in February she was writing not more than 35 words a minute. Two months later she wrote 78 words a minute in a contest at the Business Show in Boston. I have been assured by the gentleman under whose direction she was trained that the increase from 35 to 78 words a minute in less than two months was accomplished simply through the elimination of two bad habits in operating which she had acquired in school. Seven months later she won the Novice Contest at 114 words a minute. This was accomplished by the application of the efficiency principles I have already outlined, followed by intensive practice under the direction of a man who had made a special study of time studies and motion studies. Apply these principles to the study of shorthand and similar results will be achieved.

We now come to the question of how the plan may be applied, how the stu-

dent may be trained to the utmost facility in dealing with the common material, the frequent words and combinations. I believe that the only way to do this is to give systematic shorthand penmanship drill in connection with the daily instruction on the theory. This should be supplemented by a drill in correct position, correct methods of handling the pen, the notebook, and the making of rapid transitions between words or phrases, and in turning the pages of the notebook. It is of the very greatest importance that *correct habits* be established at the beginning of the work.

A Lesson from Penmanship

Here I should like to direct your attention to the great change that has taken place in the teaching of penmanship. Many of you will remember that a few years ago the copybook method of teaching the subject was in almost universal use. To-day in the best schools — the schools that are getting the best results in teaching rapid business writing — it is conspicuous by its absence. The old copybook plan was to set an engraved copy and require the students to imitate it, writing the copy slowly and painfully in a circumscribed space. There was no freedom, no life to the work, and when the student attempted to write without a copy his penmanship became a miserable scrawl.

It is a singular thing that while the copybook method is almost universally condemned by up-to-date teachers of ordinary penmanship, the copybook method of teaching shorthand is still being followed in most schools.

I believe that as much of this training as possible should be given in the form of dictation because this will accustom the student to the way in which he will apply his knowledge of shorthand in actual work. It will stimulate him to write quickly and unhesitatingly. It is by putting the student under pressure that the best results are accomplished.

In the *early* practice there is need of much repetition work, as it is from repetition that skill is acquired in anything. To be valuable this repetition work must be made *interesting*, and the way to make it interesting is to give it in the form of live, enthusiastic, intensive penmanship drills, supplemented by actual dictation.

There is only one thing needed to effect this revolution in the teaching of shorthand, and that is a real appreciation of its value by teachers and then the determination to carry it into effect. Let me say that while there is no more interesting subject to teach than shorthand, the carrying out of the plan I have outlined will enhance the interest and pleasure of the work tenfold.